YOU'RE BETTER THAN THAT!

Real Talk For Single Ladies Who Want God's Best

Rebecca Simmons

Diligence Publishing Company
Bloomfield, New Jersey

The Scripture in this book is from the King James Version and the New International Version.

YOU'RE BETTER THAN THAT!

Real Talk For Single Ladies Who Want God's Best

To contact Rebecca Simmons to preach or speak at your church, organization, seminar or conference email: powerintheword1@yahoo.com

YOU'RE BETTER THAN THAT!

Real Talk For Single Ladies Who Want God's Best

ISBN: 978-0-9963833-8-7

Printed in the United States

TABLE OF CONTENTS

DEDICATION

All honor and glory go to my Lord and Savior Jesus Christ.

This book is dedicated to my mother who has always poured out wisdom and instruction for me to follow. Mom, you are my hero. You truly are the wind beneath my wings.

To my biological daughters, Hakida Thomas and Kayla Simmons. I am so proud of you two beautiful, precious jewels that God has entrusted to me to bring into this world. God has great plans in store for you. Remember who you are. Remember to accept only God's best. Never settle for less.

To my granddaughters, Niala, Sudani, and Nairobi. I am so proud to be called "Grandma" by you three precious, beautiful young ladies. You are all destined for greatness, and it shall come to pass. Always know your value. Never allow yourself to be treated beneath your worth.

To my sisters, Janice (RIP), Rasheedah, Jackie, Renee, Christie, and my sister-in-love, Vonda. You ladies are my inspiration to keep going and to keep doing what God has called me to do. I thank God for each and every one of you and the love and support that you give me. I am so glad to be connected to you all as family. You are all beautiful, gifted and so valuable to me.

To my spiritual niece, Erica Anderson. Erica, I am so proud of you and I thank God for the day He brought us into each other's lives. You said God sent me for you, but I also know that He sent you for me. Thank you for being a constant voice of support, love, and appreciation in my life. I truly do love you.

To my female friends. I won't start naming, but you all know who you are. Thank you for being in my corner and always pushing me forward and encouraging me in all that I do for the Lord.

To my spiritual daughters and the women that I serve as Pastor. Thank you for obeying God and trusting me and Pastor Anthony with your spiritual well-being. I am blessed to be called your spiritual "Mom" and/or your "Pastor."

To women everywhere of all ages, races, sizes, shapes, and shades. You are all truly beautiful, wonderfully and fearfully made, created in the image of God.

To all of you, remember this: You are worthy to be honored and respected. You are worthy of God's best. You are better than to settle for just any old thing. You are better than that.

CHAPTER ONE

You Are Not A "B" Or A Hoe

What is the deal? We turn on the T.V. and women are being called the "B" word and hoes. I even hear beautiful women calling each other the "B" word. These women are not even fighting with each other. They are so-called friends! The last time I looked in the dictionary, the "B" word was a female dog, also a vulgar, derogatory slur for a female, and a hoe was a garden tool or a prostitute (ho).

Then we take it a little further and act like it is okay for a man to call a woman outside of her name as long as he takes ownership of her as his woman. Well, I'm here to tell you, the devil is a liar! You are not what they call you if they are calling you a "B" or a hoe or anything negative outside of your name. You are not to be defined by some obscene or derogatory term. You are created in the image of God, and what that simply means is that you are worthy of honor and respect. You are not to be cursed or identified by curse words. You are blessed!

Just because a man wraps his arms around you while he calls you these disrespectful names, does not make it right. He might even say that you're his B****# and tell you that he loves you, but Just think ahead to the when he will get mad at you. His lips will probably snarl in disgust as he hurls the same words that he spoke so sweetly to you only moments, hours, or days before. Now the whole meaning and intent has changed, and he is no longer holding you close against his chest and stroking your hair.

There is an old saying, "a rose is a rose is a rose." That's sweet, but if you take it and apply it to the "B" word or hoe (ho), it isn't so sweet. Now it's offensive. Under no circumstances should you allow yourself to be called these names.

Your man or any man that you allow in your space should call you what you are. He should call you queen. He should call you princess. He should call you beautiful. He should call you sweetheart. He should call you precious or anything along those lines that is endearing and respectful. If he calls you anything else, let him know that it is not acceptable. If he refuses to change his language, then it's up to you to kick him to the curb. He doesn't deserve to be with you. Move him out of the way so that when Mr. Right comes along, Mr. Wrong won't be blocking the path.

By the same token, you can't be acting like a female dog, a "B" or a woman who is easy to be had by anybody who wants to jump on and off of her. You must conduct yourself in a way that is worthy of the identity for which you were created. Carry yourself like a lady and you will be treated like one. Others will respect you when you respect yourself enough to hold yourself accountable to a higher level of values and standards. When people respect you, they won't call you outside of your name.

Take a stand today and refuse to allow anyone to call you names that signify a female dog, a nasty loose woman, or a prostitute. These names are disrespectful to you as a woman. You deserve to be talked to better than that. You deserve to be treated better than that. You are indeed, better than that.

Think About It!

Reflection: How does this chapter speak to me directly or indirectly?

Journal: Have I allowed myself to be talked down to or called names like B****# and Hoe by my female friends or men that I have been in relationship with?

Journal: If so, why has this been acceptable to me?

Journal: What are some of the things that I can do to change the way people see me?

Journal: What are some of the things that I can do to change the way people treat me?

Journal: What can I do to change the way people talk to me?

CHAPTER TWO

Wonderfully And Fearfully Made

You are wonderfully and fearfully made. What does that mean? It means that God outdid Himself when He created you. You are all of that, a bag of chips, some starburst, a diet coke, and some Tic-Tacs.

You've got to know it. You need to know and keep it in the forefront of your mind that you are beautiful, precious, royalty, a treasure, and worthy of the best that life has to offer. No more hiding in the shadows. Step out into the limelight and take hold of all that life has in store for you. You don't have to walk with your head down. Hold your head up and allow the world to behold your beauty. Every hair on your head is numbered. All of your features were etched out by God. The curve of your hips and the pout of your lips were all fashioned by a Master Crafter.

God knew what He was doing when He created you. You are no mistake. You are wonderfully and fearfully made. The next time you look in the mirror, don't frown and pick apart every feature that you don't like. Don't turn from side to side checking out the fact that you've gained a few pounds. The next time you look in the mirror, thank God for making you in His image. Thank Him for making you so beautiful, so precious and so unique.

There is no one like you on this earth. You are a one of a kind creation. When the Potter made you, He really did break the mold. Take pride in the fact that you cannot be successfully imitated or duplicated. No one can beat you at being you.

Dare to be yourself and not what others expect you to be.

Learn to be comfortable in your own skin. People will often try to talk down to you in order to get you to fit into their little boxes. But you don't have to go along with the program.

You see. The secret is in knowing who you are. The secret is in knowing that you are a special creation and knowing that you are indeed wonderfully and fearfully made. You don't have to accept what other people say about you.

So the next time someone calls you something derogatory or says you're too fat or too skinny, too tall or too short, or they tell you that your nose is too wide or too narrow, or that your mouth is too big, or that your lips are not big enough; the next time someone tells you that you're not pretty, or that you're not smart enough, just draw back your shoulders, stand up straight, put your hands on your hips and tell them that they had better act like they know that you are wonderfully and fearfully made and if they don't know, they better ask somebody (excuse the slang). You don't have to take people putting you down in order to manipulate you or make themselves feel better, you don't have to take that. You're better than that.

Think About It:

Reflection: How does this chapter speak to me directly or indirectly?

Journal: How do I feel about myself?

Journal: Do I find myself hiding in the shadows of life or holding myself back from happiness and success? In what ways?

Journal: Do I pick myself apart or criticize myself when I look in the mirror? What am I most critical of?

Journal: Do I have a habit of picking the wrong men to talk to or be in relationship with? Is this a reflection of how I see myself?

Journal: Do I try too hard to fit in and be like other people? What can I do about this?

Journal: Do I care too much about what other people think about me? How can I change this?

Journal: *(Write and say this out loud):* I am wonderfully and fearfully made. I am beautiful. I don't need to change to please others. I love me just the way I am. I will not let anyone put me down or make me feel less than what my value is. I am valuable. I am royalty.

CHAPTER THREE

Don't Settle For Less

Why do we as women sometimes settle for "Mr. Right Now" instead of holding out for "Mr. Right?"

Often, we go ahead and get into a relationship with the first halfway decent looking man (or not) who pays any special attention to us. Never mind the fact that he hasn't had a job in a year or that he acts like a complete jerk sometimes. Too many times, we as women, end up with men who don't deserve the time of day from us. To put it bluntly, far too many of us are settling for less in our relationships

Take a moment to think about the man in your life right now. See if he can pass this test. Take a piece of paper and number it from 1 to 22. Then answer each question by writing "Yes" if it's true about your man and "No" if it's false. Give him one point for each "Yes" answer.

Litmus test to see if he's the one for me. Answer Yes or No for each question.

1. He is a man who loves God.
2. He has a pretty good relationship with his mother.
3. I like the way he treats me when we are together.
4. He calls me more than I call him.
5. I have his home number (if he has one) and his cell phone number.
6. He keeps no secrets from me.
7. He is not married or dating someone else.
8. He talks openly to me about what's going on in his life.
9. He is sometimes romantic.
10. He offers to pay when we go out on dates.
11. He has good values.
12. I trust him around other women.
13. He spends time with me both during the week and on weekends.
14. He tells me how much he likes or loves me.
15. He gives me compliments.
16. He is kind.
17. He has never lied to me.

18. He has never grabbed me roughly or hit me.
19. He has never called me out of my name in a derogatory way.
20. His friends and family respect him.
21. He wants to get married one day.
22. He is committed to me in a one-on-one, exclusive relationship where it is clear that I am his woman.

Write down the score. If he scored between 17 and 22, this may be a good connection, 17 being on the low end and you will have to work a little harder to make your relationship work. If you gave him a "No" for anything other than number 4, 8, 9, 15, or 20, you may want to reconsider spending time with this man.

I don't know about you, but in my book, all of the above things must be true for a good relationship. If the man that you're dating fails this test, you may want to reconsider and ask yourself – "Is he the one?" Another good question is "Does he qualify to be the one?" If he is saved and loves God, yes, he could very well qualify, but only if he is the husband that God has in store for you. If he is not saved, he is not the one (At least definitely not right now). An unsaved man will not be able to walk in agreement with you on how God has ordained for you to be treated. In order for any relationship to work, you must at least be on the same page spiritually. If you love God and submit to His Word and He loves God and submits to His Word, you are equally yoked. You are walking in agreement, and you have a better chance of making your relationship and later your marriage work.

All relationships do not lead to marriage. Two people have to agree that marriage is the goal in their relationship. Note that the person that you are dating or want to date, has to want to get married and he has to want to get married to you.

If you have been dating a man for more than two years, and he has not mentioned marriage, uh oh. It is time to throw some serious hints or just come out and ask him what his intentions are. If he is not marriage minded and you are, then your relationship is out of balance, and it would perhaps be better for you if you became single minded as far as this individual is concerned and kick brother man to the curb or at least take some time apart so that you can both evaluate where you are and where you are going. Time apart from him will help you to reassess your value and redetermine what you want and deserve out of life and your relationships. Let me give you a hint. You deserve better than to be treated like someone's lifetime girlfriend or to be a "convenience" girl. You're better than that.

Think About It!

Reflection: How does this chapter speak to me directly or indirectly?

Journal: Do I settle for less in my relationships?

Journal: What is the score of the man that I'm seeing, talking to or in a relationship with on the test from pages 20-21? Did he pass the test? In what areas does he need improvement?

Journal: What are the intentions of the person that I am talking to or dating? What does he want from me? Is he marriage minded?

Journal? What can I do differently in my relationships to ensure I am not wasting my time in a relationship that's not going anywhere?

CHAPTER FOUR

Somebody Else's Guy

Tell me. How do we get caught up in relationships with somebody else's guy or somebody else's husband? Men can pretend to be pretty clueless about some things pertaining to women (no offense intended), but when it comes time for an occupied or a married man to get a woman into bed with him, it turns out that the man is not so clueless after all. Actually, men are pretty darned slick when it comes to getting us in a position that's most beneficial to them, if you know what I mean.

But what is it about us as women that makes us allow ourselves to be used by these predators? And please don't give me that, "I'm getting something out of it too" line. Please. If you even think this, you are being deceived. The devil really is a liar! You are losing way more than you think you are gaining! You are losing your dignity, your identity as a royal priesthood and your standing of favor with God.

WARNING! Leave that woman's man or husband alone! He is lying to you. He is not going to leave her for you. He is not moving out. He *is* still having sex with her. He *does* still love her. He is lying. He is cheating. He is a lying, cheating, dog!

That's right. I said it. If a man has the nerve to come to you and try to take you out, or get your phone number, or get in your IM, or DM, or get into your panties and he has a woman or a wife, he is no good and good for nothing. Just think. If he will lie to her and cheat on her, he will do the same thing to you! Run. Don't walk, but run away from this type of man. He is not your man. He is somebody else's guy.

I am not bashing men. I am bashing married men who cheat on their wives, and men who are involved in relationships who try to go out and have another woman on the side. Listen, I don't care how much money he spends on you or how many fancy places he takes you to. I don't care how much jewelry he buys you or how many gifts he gives you. If you sneak around in a relationship with a married man, you are stooping to a very low level. If you play around with somebody else's guy, you are cheapening your precious value. You are allowing yourself to become a side chick, a mistress or a booty call to a married man or a man that already has a woman! Do not allow yourself to be gotten so cheaply. You are better than that.

Think About It!

Reflection: How does this chapter speak to me directly or indirectly?

Journal: How do I feel about being in a relationship with someone who is married?

Journal: How do I feel about being in a relationship with someone who is talking to or dating someone else?

Journal: Am I willing to take the challenge and make the commitment to myself not to settle for being a side chick, a mistress or a booty call?

Journal: (*Write and say this sentence out loud):* I will not allow myself to be a side chick, a mistress, or a booty call. I will not willingly share my man or settle for being with somebody else's guy or husband.

CHAPTER FIVE

To Marry Or Not To Marry

Marriage is a good thing. If you are going to spend any serious time with the opposite sex, the idea is that the relationship should lead to marriage. I hope that you have taken the time to take your man through my little litmus test in Chapter 3. If he failed, I pray that you took the appropriate actions. If he didn't fail, then why not look forward to getting married to him one day?

Marriage is honorable and ordained by God. It was part of the Master plan from the beginning of time for one woman to be married to one man for all of their adult lives from the day of their wedding, until death do them part. Marriage can be beautiful if you manage to get hooked up with the right person. On the other hand, it can be a nightmare if you go ahead and marry a man that you know is wrong for you.

So many times, we as women make the mistake of avoiding the warning signs. If he hits you or curses you out, guess what? He is not the one. If he does not or will not work, you've got the wrong man. If he has already failed at several marriages, this is a warning sign. He is the common denominator! Either he keeps picking the wrong woman or he is the wrong man. This is another sign: If he doesn't want to spend time with you, guess what? After he marries you, he'll spend even less time with you.

Sister girl, watch the warning signs Don't marry a man who is not worthy of the time of day from you. Don't be fooled by temporary actions on his part to reel you in and get you to walk down that aisle. Talk to his family. Talk to his friends and colleagues and see if he is consistent in his behavior. How does he treat you? Is he mean to his mother or his sisters or the other women in his life (relatives and platonic friends)? Is he a flirtatious sort of guy who flirts with all the ladies? Does he have a hot, explosive temper?

Warning! Warning! Warning! All of these are caution and/or stop signs. If he treats you nice but treats everyone else badly, then chances are he's faking it, and it won't be long before you're getting the same treatment as everyone else. It generally takes about 90 days to get to know someone. I often say that when people first meet you, they will put their best foot forward; especially in a relationship. What you see is not always what you get! Take time to get to know the person that you want to date or are dating so that you will not be surprised or disappointed.

On the other hand, if your man is kind, generous, thoughtful, honest, hardworking, God fearing, patient, and gentle, then he is probably a keeper. I say, if he passes the litmus test, marry him before he gets away!

But, of course, there's always the question of whether or not he thinks you are the one for him. On the other hand, if he is an overall great guy but has no interest in marriage, I hate to be the one to tell you, but you are wasting your time. He is not marriage material; and if you stay with him, you will spend the rest of your life in a relationship with a man who does not cherish you enough to do the honorable thing and make you his wife.

Finally, you may be the one who's holding out and not wanting to be married. If this is the case, chances are you don't think that you deserve to be a wife. You may not feel worthy. I've been there, done that, got the T-shirt. However, you must come to the realization that you are worthy. According to God and His Word, when the right man discovers you as his wife, he has found a good thing *(Proverbs 18:22)*. Marriage does not make you a good thing you are already a good thing.

In spite of what you have done or what has happened in your past, you are still valuable and precious in God's sight, and you should be considered to be so in your own sight and in the sight of the person that you choose to love. You should see yourself as valuable enough to be that good thing that brings blessings to the life of the man that is smart enough to see your true value.

Whatever has happened to you does not invalidate you. Whatever you've done in life does not invalidate you. You are valuable. You don't have to settle for being someone's girlfriend for the rest of your life. You are better than that.

Think About It:

Reflection: How does this chapter speak to me directly or indirectly?

Journal: Is the relationship that I am in possibly leading to marriage?

Journal: Do I like the guy I'm dating enough to one day marry him?

Journal: Do I feel valued in the relationship that I am in right now?

Journal: Do I have a habit of picking the wrong men to talk to or be in relationship with or letting the wrong men pick me? Why? How can I change this?

Journal: Do I feel like I am worthy of the love of a good man? Why or why not?

Journal: Do I gravitate towards bad boys and push away the good ones? Why? What can I do differently to break this cycle?

Journal: (*Write and say this out loud*): I am worthy of the love of a good man. I will no longer settle for being in relationship with men that do not value me and treat me with respect. I am worthy of love, honor and respect.

CHAPTER SIX

Who's Fooling Who?

In the last section, I talked about marriage. There may be someone reading this book who is thinking, "Who needs to get married?" or "Why does everyone feel like a woman has to be married?"

I can relate to that. For many years, the last thing I wanted to do was get married. But I came to the realization one day that I wanted to be special enough to someone for him to want me to be his wife for the rest of his life.

I got tired of being in relationship after relationship. I didn't want another boyfriend. I wanted a husband. This was only after I found out that fornication (sex outside of marriage) was a sin and that God didn't approve of it one bit (although I did). After all, who was it hurting?" As a matter of fact, it didn't hurt at all. Sometimes it even worked to take away the hurt.

Oh yes, I used sex as a medicine to see if I could help myself to feel better from some of my hidden pain. (We'll talk more about that later). But the reality of it was that I was heading for danger. I could have gotten A.I.D.S. out there and died. I could have had a lot of baby daddies and babies that I would have had to raise without the father or fathers, and on a spiritual level, I was jeopardizing my future and joining myself to too many people by partaking in unmarried sex because every time we have sex with someone we are becoming one with that person and creating soul ties *(1 Corinthians 6:16)*.

But I couldn't see that. I was in darkness and couldn't see the light. Nor did I know that I was better than that. I was better than being someone's girlfriend for a year or two and not being treated like I deserved to be treated. I was better than the man in my life not wanting me enough to put a ring on my finger. I was better than that.

When I got that realization, my husband found me, and we were married. I've been married for over 22 years now. It hasn't been easy, but I wouldn't trade it for anything in the world.

You may even be thinking, "Well all I need is someone to go out with sometimes. I'm my own woman. I can take care of myself. I can pay my own bills. I don't need to get married. I just need companionship. I just need me some loving every now and then."

In reply to that, I say this to you, "Who's fooling who?"

What you're talking about is not God's plan for you. That's not God's will and it certainly is not God's best. You're better than that. You don't have to settle for less than God's best in your relationships. Allow yourself to receive the fact that your body was not created for the pleasure of a man or men who don't think enough of you to make the ultimate commitment to you and marry you. Nor was your body created for your own pleasure alone. It was created for procreation and for the pleasure of sex with your husband.

Stop giving men who are not your husband the best part of yourself. Save yourself for the man that will honor you and treasure you and make you his wife for life.

Who's fooling who? Don't believe the hype. You do deserve better than to settle for less than total commitment from the man that you love. You are better than that.

Think About It:

Reflection: How does this chapter speak to me directly or indirectly?

Journal: Am I holding myself back from getting married? Why?

Journal: Do I use sex as a medicine to cover some of the painful areas in my life?

Journal: Do I have any fears or insecurities about getting married?

Journal: If so, what are they?

CHAPTER SEVEN

Let's Talk About Sex

From the beginning of the world, it was never intended for a man or a woman to have more than one sex partner. Sex is a part of life, and a part of many intimate relationships. However, it is God's ideal for a man and a woman who are involved in sexual intimacy to be married to each other.

Aside from the fact that this is God's plan for sex, let's look at some other reasons why we don't need to be fooling around with this boyfriend/girlfriend getting busy with each other in the bedroom, hookups, or sex outside of marriage thing.

The number one reason is A.I.D.S. and/or H.I.V. The more sexual partners you have, the more potential there is for you to be infected with this life-threatening disease; although you can get it with just one sexual encounter. Then you have other STD's that are pretty nasty but not necessarily deadly such as, Herpes (which is incurable), genital warts, V.D., Chlamydia, the Clap, and Crabs (crabs are disgusting little bugs crawling in your pubic area).

Most of the time when you have sex, the lights are out and even with lights on, you can't see that someone is carrying a sexually transmitted disease. Some are curable. Some are not. All of them make it pretty embarrassing to go to the doctor to get treatment and even worse, to have to go back and tell someone that you had sex with that you have a STD and they need to go and get themselves checked out and be treated as well. Note: Condoms are not protection for some of these STD's. Also, do keep in mind that condoms sometimes break or slip off during sex.

Then we have unwanted pregnancy. Although babies are a blessing from God, too many babies are being raised by single parents (normally the mother). The welfare rolls are bulging, and the poverty level is rising (this is not to condemn a single mother, because I was a single mother once myself). This is not the time to have a baby without the advantage of a husband. It is hard enough to take care of yourself, let alone the fact that if you have a baby without being married, there is a chance that you will have to struggle to raise a child on your own. This can happen with marriage also, as marriages do break up, but if you get married and get married to the right person before getting pregnant, at least you start out ahead of the game as opposed to ending up pregnant unexpectedly by someone that you barely know or someone that has refused to make a life-long commitment to you through marriage.

As I mentioned, I've done the single parenting thing, and although my daughter was and continues to be a blessing, raising her as a single mother was hard. Being a single mother was not fun! I struggled financially and emotionally while raising my daughter on my own.

Life often changes drastically once your children start being born. When you have a baby too soon or without the support of a husband, you will often have to put your goals, education, and plans for life on hold and do whatever you have to do to take care of your child or children. God has a better plan than for you to struggle as a single mom, and abortion is not God's option; so great caution should be taken in order for you not to end up with an unwanted pregnancy.

Another reason not to have sex outside of marriage is that fornication (sex outside of marriage) is wrong in God's eyes.

While we're dealing with the spiritual aspect of unmarried sex, I want to talk about spiritual connections. It was God's intention that when a man and a woman lay down to have sex with each other, they would become one flesh, and they were not to be separated except by death of one of the two.

Since the fall of man, humans have violated God's sovereign plan for sex. We go around and have sex with whoever we want to, and we even dare to take it one step further and have sex with members of the same sex. This too, (homosexuality) is wrong in God's eyes. Society says it's okay to have sex with whoever you want to have sex with. God says it's not. Your choice depends on who is forming and shaping your life...society or God.

Then you have the crazy people who want to lay down and have sex with animals (bestiality). What the...? What in the world are they thinking about?

Nonetheless, all of this kind of sex is wrong; sex between an unmarried man and woman (fornication), sex between two people where one or both of them is married to someone else (adultery), sex between two men, sex between two women, sex in groups (orgies), sex between a man or a woman and any animal – all wrong in God's eyes. The only time that sex is acceptable in the eyes of God is when it is between a man and a woman who are married to each other. Period.

You know that we know that, especially those of us who are Christians, but we still dare to go and have some unmarried sex or some gay sex. God is not pleased when we do this! In addition to that, every time you lay down to have sex with someone, you are making a spiritual exchange. You are attaching yourself to whatever is attached to them. That's why you will find yourself acting strange after you have had sex with someone. You are acting strange because you have picked up strange spirits. You have picked up the spirit or spirits that were on the person you had sex with and they picked up what was on you. You made an even or in most cases, uneven spiritual exchange. Yes, spirits transfer, and sex is one way that they use to get from one person to the next. If the person you sleep with is crazy, depressed, or confused, you may also find yourself acting crazy, depressed and confused, because you opened yourself up and allowed those spirits to come in.

Also, when you have sex with someone, you are joining yourself spirit to spirit to that person to become one flesh. And every time you break up with a person, you are ripping apart a part of yourself in order to separate from them.

That's why it hurts so much to break up with someone, especially if you're having sex with that particular person. You are spiritually connected, and it was intended for you to stay together forever. That's why it's better to date for a few months to a year, two at the most, get married, and then have sex. That is God's ideal. Somehow, we keep missing the ideal and ending up way over in left field somewhere.

Now don't get me wrong. Not having sex as a single person in today's society is hard. Your body will talk to you, and I even had one person tell me that her body hurts due to her lusting for some sex with a certain person. That's when you have to really bring your flesh under subjection and under the power of God. Pray, read your Bible, call a friend (one that you're not sexually attracted to), exercise, take a cold shower, watch a funny PG rated movie (with no love scenes), read a book, play video games, or whatever it takes to get your mind off sex! In all of this, do not underestimate the power of God to keep you. Pray and ask God to take away the urges that are hitting your body, and He will. God will take away the urge. God is a keeper, my sister. He will keep you if you want to be kept.

Let me challenge you. Why don't you make a decision to stay sexually pure (celibate) until you get married? Save the most sacred part of yourself for the man who loves you enough to walk down the aisle and say, "I do." Don't have sex with another person until you are married to the man that God has ordained for you to be married to.

Put boundaries around yourself so you don't get caught in compromising positions that will lead to your having sex. Don't answer those late night phone calls or DM's from people looking for a booty call or DM sex (if there's such a thing. In my day, it was phone sex. I hear now, they're doing it in the DM – say it ain't so!). Don't be alone in a house or behind closed doors with someone of the opposite sex, or the same sex who is homosexual or bisexual. Don't drink and do drugs because they lower your inhibitions and you will find yourself doing things drunk or high that you would never do sober and feeling bad about it later.

Shut the door on the devil and don't give him an opportunity to make you fall. Save yourself for God's best! You deserve better than to just go from man to man and bed to bed or relationship to relationship where you keep giving away the most precious piece of yourself. You're better than that.

Think About It:

Reflection: How does this chapter speak to me directly or indirectly?

Journal: How big a part does sex play in my relationships?

Journal: Do I feel like I am playing myself cheap by having sex in my relationships? Why or why not?

Journal: Is having sex making things better or worse for me emotionally? How?

Journal: How can I conduct myself differently when it comes to sex?

Journal: Am I willing to take the challenge to abstain from sex until I am married?

Journal: *(Write and say this out loud):* I do not have to have sex to get or keep a man. I desire to stay sexually pure until I am married. I will pray about taking the challenge to remain celibate until I am married.

When you are ready to take the challenge, write and say this out loud:

I will remain celibate until I get married. The next person I have sex with will be my husband.

Signature:

Date:

CHAPTER EIGHT

What Is Your Problem?

The last few chapters may have provoked mixed emotions for you as you read them. The truth is that not everyone wants to get married and not everyone can abstain from fulfilling their sexual needs in a relationship. I can dig it (I guess I'm telling my age here. LOL).

The truth of the matter is that I was far from attaining this myself. Primarily, because I had too many issues to get this one right (although near the end of my single years, I tried very hard to save myself for marriage). My issues were so big that I had an impossible time of this being a new believer in Christ. I only wish that someone had helped me to deal with my insecurities or that I had given my life to God earlier in my life.

I had this learned behavior that taught me that the only way to get and keep a man was to go to bed with him and do the nasty (There I go telling my age again). The devil is a liar! I know now that a man respects a woman more when she values herself enough to say no when he starts to pressure her for sex. I also know now that when a woman says no, a real man backs up and respects her wishes. But again, I learned this lesson a little late.

I was molested when I was a child, and I always thought that if I had sex with a man, then he would like me or that he would love me. I also believed that if I told him no, he wouldn't like me. So, every relationship that I had, we eventually ended up having sex. As a result of this, I went through a lot of pain in my life, carrying the spiritual residue of my past and what had happened to me from one relationship to the next; Not to mention the fact that I was violating God's wishes by having unmarried sex. But, I am grateful that I started to realize that I was better than that.

I finally learned that it was better to hold out and wait for the man who would marry me. I became less desperate and less giving and one day, I met a man who respected me and valued me enough to do the right thing.

I'm not talking about getting married to any man. I'm talking about getting married to the right man. I'm talking about getting married to your soul mate. You must not be desperate or insecure about your value and marry the first man who asks you to marry him or who agrees to marry you, and you can't marry a man just because you want to have sex with him. You must know beyond a shadow of a doubt that this man is the one for you. Again, my test in Chapter 3 is a good way to gauge if he is marriage material or not.

But what if you're the problem like I was? What if you've got issues? The molestation left me broken, bruised, angry, insecure, and feeling dirty and unworthy of the love of a good man. I felt that no one would want me after what had happened, so I settled for all of the wrong men that came along in my life. I was angry and wanted to make every man pay for what had happened to me, so my relationships didn't last long. I was ashamed of my past, so I didn't push too hard to be treated right in my relationships.

What was my problem? I had issues. That's what my problem was. But I faced my issues, and now they are behind me. With God's help, I forgave the person who molested me. I accepted the fact that I was worthy of being treated right in my relationships, and I no longer allowed myself to be in relationships with the wrong people.

So, what's your problem? Whatever your problem is, you don't have to let it defeat you or make you think you don't deserve a good life or a good relationship and or marriage. You don't have to live your life angry, broken, or hurting. You don't have to live bound up by anger and un-forgiveness. You don't have to be scared or insecure. You don't have to have sex with people just to feel loved and accepted. You are loved and accepted by God. You are valuable and precious. You are more precious than rubies. You don't have to sabotage your relationships or fear being rejected. You don't have to settle for less. My sister, you don't have to take nobody's mess because you're better than that!

Think About It:

Reflection: How does this chapter speak to me directly or indirectly?

Journal: What is my problem? What issues do I have that are standing in the way of my happiness?

Journal: Do I value myself enough to not have sex with everyone who tries to have sex with me?

Journal: Am I insecure or afraid of not being accepted? What is the remedy for this?

Journal: Am I using sex to get or keep a man?

Journal: Do I have feelings of anger that I need to deal with? Is there someone that I need to forgive because of something that happened to me when I was a child or even in later years? What and who are they?

Journal: Do I sabotage my relationships? If so, why?

Journal: *(Write and say this out loud):* I will not hold on to anger and unforgiveness. I forgive everyone who has hurt me in my past.

Journal: *(Write and say this out loud):* I am loved and accepted by God. I am more precious than rubies. I will not have sex with a person just to feel loved or to get a man. I will not sabotage my relationships. I will not fear rejection. I will not settle for less. I will take no mess. I am better than that!

CHAPTER NINE

No More Shame, No More Guilt

Too often, we let shame and guilt prevent us from having all that we could have in life. Shame and guilt will prevent us from having good relationships and good health. Shame and guilt can contaminate every aspect of our lives. That is why we must extract the poison of shame and guilt from our lives.

As I mentioned in the last chapter, I was molested when I was a young girl. As a result, I carried a lot of shame because this thing had happened to me and guilt because I never really told anyone. I also felt guilty because I thought that this act of molestation was actually my fault.

For years, I displayed disruptive behaviors because of my feelings of shame and guilt. I started drinking and doing drugs. I allowed an older boy to talk me into giving him my virginity. Actually, he took it, because once I found myself in this compromising position, I tried to stop him, but he wouldn't stop, and he went ahead and had sex with me against my will. I got pregnant by this boy and ended up losing my baby. I started spiraling downward even the more so after this. I had been a straight "A" student, but I started cutting school. I got pregnant again at 15, became a mother at 16, and because I let pride get in my way and didn't want to go to summer school after 12th grade to get my diploma, I dropped out of high school in the middle of 12th grade!

I ended up on welfare and in one bad relationship after another. I constantly kicked men out of my life because I was afraid of what they would think if they knew what had happened to me when I was a little girl. I didn't let any of them get too close to me because I feared being rejected by them. As a result of my fear of revealing the secret me and letting people know the real me, I ended up living my life as a phony and spent a lot of time being lonely.

Eventually, I got sick and tired of being sick and tired, and I let this guy that I met in the bar one night talk me into going to church. There, I found the answer to my problems. When I heard about Jesus and the love that God has for me, my life began to make a very slow turn for the better.

By the time I had visited my new friend's church for the third time, I was convinced that the answer to my problems would be found in church or in the Bible.

I found out that I was wonderfully and fearfully made. I found out that God loves me so much that He sent His son Jesus to die for me. I found out that God has a great plan for my life and that it was for good and not for evil. I found out that I didn't have to live with the shame and the guilt. I found out that the molestation was not my fault. That was the biggest revelation of my life. It was not my fault.

In the same way, it is not your fault if you were molested or even if you were raped. There was nothing that you did to bring that upon yourself, and there was nothing you could have done to stop it. You were not too pretty, too fast, too sexy. You did not ask for it. You did not seduce him (or her). You could not make it stop. Yes, you could have told that somebody had hurt you or had sex with you against your will, but you were probably scared. You were a victim. If you were molested when you were a child, the person probably threatened you that if you told, they would blame you, or hurt you, or kill you or somebody that you loved. They probably said that if you told, they would say it was your idea and your fault.

I have a newsflash for you. You are not to blame. It was not your fault. You were only a child, and you should not even have had this thing happen to you. Even if you told or did not tell, it was not your fault. Even if it felt good or you enjoyed it or after a while started looking forward to it, it was not your fault. You may even feel guilty because you enjoyed it a little, or a lot. Don't. One of the tactics of child molesters (pedophiles) is to make the victim feel as good and as comfortable as possible while they do what they do. They don't want to bring their victims pain. Some perpetrators actually get more of a thrill from this indecent act if the victim enjoys it.

So, clear yourself of any blame right now! You are not to blame. You are not dirty. You are not a slut. You are not a whore or any profane thing that you might have been called. You can beak the shame from your past if you receive this truth today. Even if you fell in love with the person who did it and acted like their girlfriend, it was not your fault. You were a child and you were taken advantage of by someone who probably should have been protecting you.

I also want to also say to that mother whose child was hurt in any way by someone and you did not know what was going on, that it was not your fault. The only error you made was in loving the wrong man or trusting the wrong person to take care of your child. You had no idea that the person was going to harm your child! Stop carrying the guilt and the shame around like a dead corpse that's controlling your life. Forgive yourself for the error of judgement. See the reality that your child being harmed was not a part of the plan that you had in mind as you entered into relationship with this person and realize that it was not your fault. This person deceived you and did you wrong too! You too, were victimized when this happened to your child. You are not to blame! Receive this word and get free today!

Also, if you are a person who had alcoholic parents, if you were physically abused, if your parents were drug addicts or in jail, if you have issues because of your not being covered by your parents, you have to grasp the fact that your parents had issues too, and their actions are not your fault. You no longer have to feel ashamed of the lives that your parents lived or be bound by their dysfunction.

The shame that does become yours is the shame that results from your doing things that can bring embarrassment to yourself and others as a result of what happened to you. In the same way, guilt becomes your guilt when you continually do things that you know are wrong.

That was my issue. The molestation was not my fault, but the way that I acted afterwards was. The sex, the drugs, the alcohol, the partying, the neglect of my responsibilities, were all my fault and I had to come to a point where I was sick and tired of the dysfunction in my life. I had to stop running from myself and deal with my issues. I had to face the facts, learn the truth and embrace that truth. I said I had to embrace the truth.

The truth was that all of the terrible things that I experienced in my life – the things that happened to me that were beyond my control – were not my fault, but the things that I did in the years following that were my fault. I had to take responsibility for those things, repent of them, and turn to God to help me to deal with my issues. That He did and continues to do. I have no more guilt and no more shame. I'm free. Thank God Almighty, I am free!

You too can be free of the shame and the guilt if you will receive the truth that the things that happened to you in life were not your fault. You were a victim, but you don't have to continue to live your life as a victim any longer! Give the guilt, the shame, the bitterness, the pain, the anger, the unforgiveness, all of it! – Give it all over to God. God can help you if you let Him. You don't have to live with the shame. You don't have to live with the guilt. You don't have to live a messed-up life filled with issues. You don't have to live like that. You're better than that.

Think About It:

Reflection: How does this chapter speak to me directly or indirectly?

Journal: Is shame and guilt holding me back or creating problems in my life? How?

Journal: How can I deal with shame and guilt because of something that was done to me?

Journal: How can I deal with shame and guilt because of something that I have done?

Journal: How can I deal with shame and guilt over something that happened to someone that I love, and I had no knowledge of what was going on?

Journal: How can I deal with shame and guilt over what my parents did or did not do?

Journal: *(Write and say this out loud):* I will no longer allow shame and guilt to rule over and ruin my life. I acknowledge that the bad things that people did to me were not my fault. I acknowledge that what someone did to my loved one without me knowing about it was not my fault. I acknowledge that I have done some wrong things in my life, and today I repent of them and turn over a new leaf. Today I am free from shame and guilt.

CHAPTER TEN

A New Creation Filled With Power

In Chapters 1 through 9, I discussed a lot of things pertaining to relationships and life. God has a great plan for your life and the only way to walk fully in those plans is to have God on your side. You must have a power greater than yourself when it comes to building your self-esteem, not settling for less, getting rid of shame and guilt, dealing with your issues, knowing and embracing your true identity and staying out of some man's bed.

Only God can keep us even when we don't feel like being kept. Only God can lift us up from our low places in life and position us to win. Only God can help us to see that we deserve better than to be somebody's woman on the down low or to have babies for, clean for, cook meals for, and wash the dirty drawers of men who refuse to marry us. Only God can show us that we're better than that.

2 Corinthians 5:17 says "Therefore if anyone is in Christ, he (she) is a new creation, the old has gone. The new has come."

This scripture is the basis of my life now. I constantly remind myself that I am a new creation. The old has gone, and the new has entered in. In order for us to be a new creation, we have to be in Christ. Being in Christ is not a confession or a walk down the aisle of a church. It's a position. It is a lifestyle.

Before Jesus came to walk the Earth, the world was filled with sin, and all humanity was cut off from being in relationship with God. God did not want things to stay that way. He wanted to be in relationship with us and besides that, He loves us so much that he was not satisfied to let us perish and to be condemned to the eternal fires of Hell. He had already given mankind options for redemption and many chances to get it right, but man abused and misused all of them, so He sent His Son Jesus Christ to die as the final sacrifice for our sins. Jesus took our sins upon Himself and died on the cross so that all who accepted Him and His sacrifice could come into right relation-ship with God; so that we could live eternally with God, and so that we would not have to pay the penalty for our sins.

The Gospel tells us that Jesus was born of a virgin, He was crucified for our sins. He died. He was buried, and on the third day, He rose from the grave. After showing His resurrected self to many people, including His disciples, He ascended into Heaven. He is seated on the right hand of the Father, and one day, He is coming back to judge the living and the dead.

In order to be born again into a new creation, we as believers have repented of our sins and accepted Jesus Christ into our lives as Lord and Savior.

If we believe with our hearts and confess with our mouths that Jesus is LORD, we are saved. At salvation, we received the indwelling of God's Holy Spirit to come and live inside of us, and we are thereby no more the old creation, but a new creation. This is the good news of the Gospel that saved and changed my life! I am so grateful for the blood of Jesus Christ that was shed for me and the power of His resurrection that has now been made available to me as a believer in Jesus Christ. God is no respecter of persons. The great news is that salvation and deliverance is available to us all.

Once we are believers through faith and confession, we receive power through God's Holy

Spirit. This power gives us the ability to overcome everything that has tried to destroy us and everything that has been sent to keep us from living an abundant life of total victory. But, even though we receive this power, it often lies dormant in the lives of believers and many continue to live defeated lives. Many stay stuck in the circumstances, behaviors, guilt, shame and cycles of their past. This is not God's will for us. God wants us to be free.

Those who are free in Christ are free indeed! If you feel stuck, even if you have been a believer for a long time, God wants to get you unstuck and moving forward into the victorious life that He ordained for you. If you need a refreshing, it's available to you today. So, whether you're feeling stuck in a cycle of sin or frustration, if you need a refreshing of God's Spirit, or if you never prayed a prayer of repentance and you want to do so, pray the following prayer out loud:

Oh God, I repent of my sins. I believe in my heart that Jesus Christ is your Son who came to die for my sins, and I receive Him today fully as Savior and LORD of my life. As a believer, I receive a fresh infilling of your Spirit to dwell in me and make me new. Refresh me oh Lord, and fill me with your power! I believe and receive that I am a new creation. I am saved. I am victorious! I am more than a conqueror! I am the head and not the tail. I am above and never beneath. I am a joint heir with Christ of the promises of Abraham. I am a royal priesthood. I release the old me and I receive the new me. From this day forth, I will walk in my new DNA. I will walk and operate according to your Kingdom. Let your will be done in my life as you have already ordained in Heaven. I receive it today. Manifest your glory now Lord, in my life. I pray this prayer in the Name of Jesus! Amen.

If you prayed this prayer with faith in your heart, you are entering into a whole new season and a new dimension in God. God is already working to manifest newness, blessings, healing and breakthrough in your life!

However, it will take time for the many things that God has in store for you to take effect and come into fruition. You must be patient and not give up on God as He works behind the scenes in your life. If you don't currently go to church, get into a Bible-believing church and go weekly to sit up under the teaching of your pastor who is appointed to help you to grow in the things pertaining to the Kingdom of God. If you do go to church, keep going! Go expecting to hear from God and see Him move in your life. Watch, pray, and wait for God to do a miraculous work in your life. God has great things in store for you!

Listen. When you have Jesus in your life, you have to realize and keep in the front of your mind that you are a new creation filled with the Dunamis (power) of God. You have the power to cast out every opposing force and demolish every stronghold that tries to bring any confusion, distraction, negativity, dysfunction, lack and shortcomings into your life. You have the power available to you to be set free from all of the hindrances of your past.

Speaking of hindrances of the past, we need to talk about forgiveness. I talked about how I forgave the person that molested me. I have also forgiven many others over the years. In order to break chains off your emotions and walk in power, you have to forgive! You have to forgive and keep forgiving the people that hurt you. Unforgiveness is a stubborn stronghold that is difficult to break. Most of the time we don't even want to forgive. We want to hold on to the anger not realizing that when we hold on to the anger, we hold on to the hurt and pain that caused the anger. We must forgive in order to be totally free.

If you are having a tough time forgiving someone, do what I did and ask God to help you to forgive all who have hurt you. It won't be easy, and you may not even want to forgive. You might feel like they don't deserve to be forgiven and all of this is true. The key is that your forgiving them will set you free from the emotional ties that have held you hostage for so many years of your old life or that will try to hold you hostage in the present or the future. You have to let go of all of the baggage that is stopping you from living your best life possible. Again, pray and ask God to help you to forgive those who have hurt you just as you being a new creation have been forgiven for all of your sins – past, present and future. There is power in forgiveness. Forgiveness is a supernatural, miraculous occurrence, and with God's help, you will receive and witness this miracle of letting go of the past so that you can embrace your glorious, joy-filled present and future. Some people will be forgiven to continue in relationship with you, but some people, you will have to forgive them and let them go!

God has total prosperity in every area of your life in store for you. Speak victory over your life today. Release your power today. Bind up every evil spirit that may be trying to destroy you today.

Decree God's blessings over your life. Speak the Word of God into manifestation in your life. The power is in your mouth! Use your power.

Don't let the enemy of your soul continue to have his way in your life. Don't spend another day angry, miserable, and discontented. Don't spend another day looking for love in all the wrong places. Don't spend another day with people who don't honor you taking up space in your life. Don't spend another day in a bad or wrong relationship. Don't spend another day thinking and believing that you don't deserve God's best in every area of your life including your relationships. As a child of God, you deserve only the best. As a daughter of Zion, God only has His best in store for you! Don't settle for less. Do not settle. Why? Because you're better than that!

Think About It:

Reflection: How does this chapter speak to me directly or indirectly?

Journal: How important is it to have God in my life and in my corner?

Journal: How much does God love me?

Journal: Am I a new creation? How do I or How did I become a new creation?

Journal: What are some of the things I can do as a new creation to bring about change in my life?

Journal: What kind of power has been given to me as a new creation?

Journal: Why do I need to forgive people who have hurt me or done me wrong?

Journal: *(Write and say this out loud):* I will not spend another day mad, miserable, discontented, looking for love in all the wrong places, in wrong relationships, or thinking or believing that I don't deserve God's best. I will not settle for less because I'm better than that!

Journal: What do you deserve as a child of God?

Journal: Why should you never settle for being treated with dishonor? Hint The answer is (Because I am better than that!)

Write down the answer below and say the answer out loud!

ABOUT THE AUTHOR

Rebecca Simmons aka Pastor Rebecca is a woman after God's own heart. She was saved from a life of destruction and unhappiness in 1994 and she has known since then that God had a better plan for her life. She also realized that the trouble and heartache that she had been through in her own life was not for nothing. Later in her Christian walk, she learned that her experiences would be used to help other women to realize that they too can overcome the pain of their pasts and walk the path of victorious living.

Pastor Rebecca is married with four children and four grandchildren. She is a Proverbs 31 wife and mother and she and her husband and children live in New Jersey, the state that she calls home although she was born in Florida. This is credited to the fact that she has lived in New Jersey for as long as she can remember.

Pastor Rebecca received certification as a Certified Christian Counselor. from the American Association of Christian Counselors in 2003. She is one of the pastors of New Creation Christian Ministries in Hillside, New Jersey where she co-pastors alongside of her husband Pastor Anthony Simmons. She ministers under a heavy prophetic anointing and was commissioned as a prophet in 2012. She acknowledges that she has been called by God to minister to the hurting, the broken, the discouraged and those individuals who are seeking "a better way."

Pastor Rebecca is also a prolific speaker and preacher who breaks the bread of wisdom concerning all aspects of the Bible, life, and relationships in a caring but no-nonsense way. She is the founder of Woman To Woman Empowerment Group and Healing For the WHOLE Woman. Both can be found on Facebook. Her personal and ministry mission is to make a positive difference in the lives of enough people to make a positive difference in the world by any means necessary!

The Lord has also led Pastor Rebecca to write another inspirational book entitled *MAN Problems*. This book addresses the issues of Molestation, Abandonment and Neglect by the fathers and the men in the lives of women everywhere. Under God's divine guidance, she has written two healing novels, *Nobody's Business* and *Daddy Love*. Both of these novels take a realistic look at relationships through the lives of fictional characters that women and men across America find themselves relating to. She has also co- written, *Kayla's Day*, a children's motivational book, with her daughter Kayla when Kayla was six years old. This book deposits basic lessons of motivation and determination into the hearts of children while they are still young.

Thereby when they are older they will not stray away from these teachings. She is the author of inspirational and motivational books, *Pump Up The Power, Get the Life You Want, Don't Die In The Wilderness, Making Marriage And Relationships Work,* and *Moving Forward When Life Lets You Down.*

ORDER INFORMATION

You can order additional copies of *You're Better Than That! Real Talk For Single Ladies Who Want God's Best* by emailing the author directly using the email address below.

Email Address:
pastorrebeccasimmons@gmail.com

Books are available at Amazon.com,
Kindle and Your Local Bookstores (By Request)

Other Books By Rebecca Simmons

MAN Problems.

Nobody's Business

Daddy Love.

Kayla's Day

The Cry Of A Woman's Heart: Healing The Pain Of The Past, Traveling The Road To Victorious Living

Making Marriage And Relationships Work

Pump Up The Power, Get the Life You Want

Don't Die In The Wilderness

Moving Forward When Life Lets You Down

Please leave a review for this book on Amazon and let other readers know how much you enjoyed reading it.

Thank you!

www.ingramcontent.com/pod-product-compliance
Lightning Source LLC
Chambersburg PA
CBHW060414050426
42449CB00009B/1970